About Me: Chris T. Risen

Hello and welcome! I'm Chris T. Risen, a seasoned professional with an extensive background in direct marketing, affiliate marketing, sales funnels, and leading dynamic sales teams. With years of invaluable experience under my belt, I've had the privilege of being a partner in one of the esteemed organizations recognized on the Inc 500 list of fastest-growing companies.

Professional Background
My journey in the dynamic field of marketing began over a decade ago, where my innate passion for connecting products with people found its true calling. Over the years, I have dedicated my skills and effort to marketing, where I've worked tirelessly to understand the intricacies and nuances that drive successful campaigns.

I've spearheaded marketing initiatives for eight distinctive brands, each with its unique identity, audience, and market position. This diversity in experience has not only broadened my perspective but also deepened my insights into the multifaceted world of marketing, making me adaptable and proficient in handling various marketing challenges and opportunities.

Expertise
Direct Marketing: With a robust background in direct marketing, I've developed and executed campaigns that directly engage the target audience, driving response and conversions through carefully crafted strategies and messages.

Affiliate Marketing: In the realm of affiliate marketing, I've worked on both sides of the spectrum—promoting products as an affiliate and driving sales through affiliates. This comprehensive experience has provided me with a deep understanding of the affiliate marketing landscape.

Sales Funnels: Mastering the art and science of sales funnels, I've successfully created and optimized conversion-focused funnels that not only attract but also retain customers, maximizing lifetime value and enhancing customer satisfaction.

Sales Teams: Leading high-performance sales teams has been one of my areas of expertise. By fostering a collaborative and motivated environment, I've guided teams to exceed sales targets while maintaining a focus on providing value to our clients and customers.

Inc 500 Fastest Growing Company Partnership: Being a partner in an Inc 500 recognized company has been a monumental milestone in my career. It is a testament to the collective hard work, innovation, and relentless pursuit of excellence that defines my approach to business and marketing.

My Approach
I approach marketing as a dynamic, evolving field that requires a blend of creativity, analytics, and an unerring focus on customer needs. In every campaign, strategy, or project I undertake, the customer is always at the core. By understanding their needs, preferences, and behaviors, I craft marketing strategies that resonate, engage, and convert.

Here's to successful marketing endeavors and the exciting journey that each campaign brings. Looking forward to crossing paths with like-minded professionals, collaborators, and enthusiasts in the field!

Chris T. Risen

Introduction

Welcome to a world of opportunities where earning passive income from the comfort of your home is not just a dream but a very attainable reality. The realm of affiliate marketing extends its welcoming hands to individuals from all walks of life, offering a platform where financial growth is fostered through simple, yet strategic online promotional activities. For beginners keen on stepping into this lucrative domain, "A Beginner's Guide to Successful Affiliate Marketing from Home: Passive Income Made Simple" is crafted just for you.

Affiliate marketing is an innovative and efficient marketing strategy in which you—the affiliate—earn commissions by promoting another's products or services. Essentially, you serve as a conduit connecting prospective buyers to the products or services they seek. You will be crafting and sharing engaging content that nudges your audience towards making purchases through your unique affiliate link, with every concluded sale via this link bringing in earnings for you.

This approach to earning is marked by its simplicity, low entry barriers, and potential for significant returns. You are not tasked with product creation, customer service provision, or order fulfillment; your sole objective is effective promotion leading to sales. With a computer, internet connection, and commitment, you can engage in affiliate marketing from anywhere, enjoying the flexibility it provides.

In the pages that unfold, this guide is set to illuminate the path of affiliate marketing for novices, providing a step-by-step walkthrough of the essential concepts and actions required to launch and sustain successful affiliate campaigns from home. You will learn about:

Understanding Affiliate Marketing: A deep dive into the mechanics of affiliate marketing to give you a clear picture of how it operates and how you can begin earning.

Benefits of Engaging in Affiliate Marketing: Exploring the myriad advantages and the allure of affiliate marketing as a dependable income source.

Navigating Through Niche Selection: Guidance on how to pinpoint and select a niche that aligns with your interests and has profitable potential.

Joining Affiliate Programs: Insights on affiliating with the right programs and businesses to ensure profitability and reliability.

Crafting Content That Converts: Tips and tricks for producing content that not only draws attention but also persuades and converts leads into sales.

With "A Beginner's Guide to Successful Affiliate Marketing from Home: Passive Income Made Simple" as your resource, you are equipped with the knowledge and strategies needed to confidently and proficiently begin your affiliate marketing adventure. Let's embark on this journey to unlock the doors to passive income together!

Step 1: How Affiliate Marketing Works

The affiliate marketing process is straightforward and can be distilled into a series of simple steps that culminate in the earning of commissions through online sales. This revenue-generating model leverages the power of recommendation and online content creation, and here, we will walk through its operational framework.

First and foremost, your journey begins with the promotion of a product or service. As an affiliate, you undertake the creation and online dissemination of content aimed at showcasing and recommending specific products or services. The canvas for your content is vast and varied, providing multiple platforms to reach your audience. From crafting insightful blog posts and creating engaging videos to making impactful social media posts, the avenues are plenty, and the choice is yours.

The content you create will house your unique affiliate link—a special URL that tracks the traffic and customers you send to the product owner's site. This link is indispensable as it is your identifier; it marks the customers coming through your promotional efforts and ensures you get the credit (and commissions) for the sales generated through your referrals.

Once your content is live and accessible, the audience engagement begins. Potential customers interact with your content, and if they find value and alignment with their needs, they would likely click on your embedded affiliate link, leading them to the product or service's official sales page. This is where the conversion process takes place, turning potential leads into paying customers.

Your role as an affiliate is pivotal yet straightforward—create content that informs, persuades, and leads to a click on your affiliate link. The ensuing sales process and customer service are handled by the product owner or merchant, relieving you of these responsibilities. Your focus remains razor-sharp: promote, lead, and earn.

The culmination of this process is the earning of commissions. For every sale completed through your affiliate link, a predetermined percentage of the sale amount (commission) is credited to you. The rate of commission varies across different affiliate programs and products, with some offering as much as 50% or more.

It's imperative to understand that affiliate marketing is not a 'get-rich-quick' scheme; it demands time, effort, and consistency. Success in this field is born out of strategic planning, creating high-quality content, and building trust with your audience. With these elements in place, the straightforward process of affiliate marketing unfolds, leading you to earn passive income from the comfort of your home.

In the following sections of "A Beginner's Guide to Successful Affiliate Marketing from Home: Passive Income Made Simple", we will delve deeper into each step, providing you with the insights and tools needed to navigate through the exciting and rewarding landscape of affiliate marketing successfully. Stay tuned and keep turning the pages!

Step 2: Benefits Of Affiliate Marketing

Affiliate marketing indisputably opens doors to an array of advantages for digital entrepreneurs, presenting an attractive alternative for earning online. From generating a passive income stream to allowing flexibility in your work life, the benefits are both promising and accessible. Below are some of the significant advantages that make affiliate marketing a go-to option for online income seekers.

Passive Income Generation

Earning while you sleep becomes a tangible reality with affiliate marketing. Once your promotional content is live and optimized, it passively attracts and guides potential customers to products or services, earning you a commission for each successful transaction, without the need for your active, continuous involvement.

Potential Monthly Earnings: $2k-$20k from Home

With the right strategies, niches, and dedication, affiliate marketing offers the potential for significant earnings, ranging from $2,000 to $20,000 per month or even more. This range isn't guaranteed and varies based on multiple factors including the products you choose to promote, the commission structure, your marketing strategies, and the effort you put in. Working from home, you can create a comfortable and potentially lucrative income stream, all depending on your commitment and the smart execution of affiliate marketing techniques.

Cost-Effective Start

Affiliate marketing demands minimal upfront investment. Unlike traditional businesses, there's no need for substantial capital to get started, as you won't create a product, stock inventory, or manage deliveries and customer service. Essentially, your initial investment boils down to a computer, internet access, and your time and effort to craft engaging content.

Flexibility and Independence

Enjoy unparalleled flexibility and independence with affiliate marketing. Freed from the conventional 9-to-5 work structure, you decide your work hours, crafting a schedule that aligns perfectly with your lifestyle and productivity peaks. This venture can be pursued from anywhere—be it your home, a café, or while traversing the globe.

Diverse Product Selection

The affiliate marketing universe is abundant with a diverse range of products and services to promote. With countless businesses and individuals offering affiliate programs, you can find and align yourself with niches that not only pique your interest but also resonate with your knowledge and passion, lending authenticity and enthusiasm to your promotional endeavors.

Low-Risk Venture

Affiliate marketing is characterized by low financial risk since you're not investing in product creation or holding inventory. Your primary investment is your time and creative effort, allowing you to explore and experiment with promoting various products without the financial anxiety tied to unsold stock or unsuccessful product launches.

Scalable Income

Your income through affiliate marketing is scalable. As you refine your skills and expand your online presence, your earning potential concurrently grows. With strategic effort and a commitment to learning and adapting, you'll find your income can increase progressively, offering a stable and expanding source of funds.

In "A Beginner's Guide to Successful Affiliate Marketing from Home: Passive Income Made Simple", the subsequent pages will guide you meticulously through each step, providing the requisite knowledge and tools to not only commence but thrive in affiliate marketing, effectively leveraging its myriad benefits for your financial gain.

Step 3: Finding The Right Niche

Identifying and settling on the right niche is a cornerstone in laying a robust foundation for your affiliate marketing journey. The niche you select significantly influences your potential earnings and the ease with which you can connect with your target audience. This section illuminates the crucial aspects of niche selection, offering tips to guide you in making an informed decision.

Why Niche Selection is Crucial

Precision Targeting: A well-defined niche enables you to create content that specifically caters to a particular group's interests and needs. Such precision in targeting facilitates effective engagement with your audience, enhancing the potential for conversions.

Expertise Development Focusing on a specific niche allows you to develop in-depth knowledge and expertise in that area. Becoming an authority in your chosen niche builds trust with your audience, a critical factor in influencing purchasing decisions.

Reduced Competition: While popular niches are lucrative, they are also highly competitive. Choosing a unique or sub-niche reduces competition, providing an easier pathway to establish yourself and succeed in the affiliate marketing space.

Tips for Choosing a Niche

Align With Your Passion or Interest: Engaging with a niche that aligns with your passions or interests makes the process enjoyable and sustainable. When you are enthusiastic about the niche, content creation becomes natural and engaging, enhancing your ability to connect with like-minded individuals.

Market Demand Analysis: A profitable niche has a steady demand in the market. Conduct market research to identify niches with potential for growth and sustainability. Tools like Google Trends, keyword planners, and market research platforms can provide valuable insights into demand dynamics.

Profitable Affiliate Programs: Ensure the niche you select has profitable affiliate programs. Look for products or services within the niche that offer attractive commission rates and have a track record of sales.

Audience Engagement: Evaluate the level of engagement within potential niches. Active and engaged communities indicate a healthy interest level, providing a ready audience for your content.

Gap Analysis: Identify gaps in the market where customer needs are unmet or inadequately addressed. Such gaps represent opportunities for you to offer value through your content and promotions.

Practical Steps for Niche Selection

1. List Your Interests: Begin by listing areas you are passionate or knowledgeable about.

2. Research: Conduct market research to assess demand, competition, and profitability in each potential niche.

3. Identify Affiliate Programs: Look for reliable and lucrative affiliate programs within each niche.

4. Analyze the Audience: Study the audience's behavior, interests, and engagement levels in each niche.

5. Select a Niche: Based on your analysis, select a niche that best aligns with your interest, market demand, profitability, and audience engagement levels.

In subsequent sections of "A Beginner's Guide to Successful

Affiliate Marketing from Home: Passive Income Made Simple", we will delve into the particulars of joining affiliate programs and crafting compelling content to ensure success in your chosen niche. These insights will further equip you to navigate through the affiliate marketing landscape effectively and profitably. Each step in this guide is a stepping stone towards realizing your potential earnings of $2k to $20k a month or more from the comfort of your home!

Step 4: Joining An Affiliate Program

After carefully selecting your niche, you're ready to take the next pivotal step in your affiliate marketing journey—joining an affiliate program. Affiliate programs serve as the bridge connecting you, the affiliate, and the merchants or product owners. They provide a structured platform where you can select products that resonate with your niche, promoting them to earn commissions on sales generated through your unique affiliate link. In this section, we'll guide you through the process of joining an affiliate program and highlight key factors to consider during this crucial stage.

How to Join an Affiliate Program

1. Research: Start by researching affiliate programs that align with your chosen niche. Look for programs that offer products or services relevant to your content and audience.

2. Apply: Once you identify a suitable program, apply to join. This process typically involves filling out a form with your personal and payment details, as well as information about your promotional strategies and platforms.

3. Get Approved: Approval might be instant or take some time, depending on the program's policies. Some programs may review your application manually to ensure you meet their requirements and standards.

4. Access Affiliate Links: Upon approval, you'll gain access to affiliate links, banners, and other promotional materials. You can start incorporating these into your content to drive traffic and sales to the merchant's site.

Key Factors to Consider

Commission Rates: Different programs offer various commission rates. Look for programs with competitive and attractive rates. Remember, higher rates don't always guarantee more income; you must also consider the product's price and sales potential.

Payment Terms: Understand the program's payment policies. How often will you be paid, and what is the payment threshold? Familiarize yourself with their payment methods as well to ensure they suit your preferences.

Cookie Duration: Cookie duration refers to the window of time during which you can earn a commission after a user clicks on your affiliate link. Longer durations increase your chances of earning.

Support: Opt for programs that offer robust support to affiliates. Good support includes access to promotional materials, timely communication, and assistance in optimizing your affiliate marketing efforts.

Reputation: Consider the reputation of the affiliate program and the merchants involved. Programs associated with trustworthy and reliable merchants tend to offer a smoother and more profitable experience.

Product Relevance: The products offered should be relevant to your niche and audience. Promoting products that align with your content and audience interests increases the likelihood of conversions and sales.

Getting Started

With these considerations in mind, start exploring various affiliate programs available in your selected niche. Compare the programs based on the outlined factors, weighing the pros and cons of each. Once you settle on a program that aligns with your goals and expectations, proceed with the application process.

Navigating through the selection and application process might seem daunting, but with due diligence and careful consideration, you'll find a program that not only fits your niche but also supports your journey towards earning $2k to $20k a month or more from home through affiliate marketing.

Stay tuned for the subsequent sections of "A Beginner's Guide to Successful Affiliate Marketing from Home: Passive Income Made Simple", where we will further demystify the process of creating compelling and converting content, among other crucial steps to fortify your affiliate marketing success. Each page turned is a step closer to mastering the art and science of affiliate marketing!

Step 5: Creating Quality Content

Content sits at the very core of affiliate marketing, serving as the primary tool to draw and engage your audience, while gently leading them towards making informed purchasing decisions through your affiliate links. Crafting content that is not just high-quality but also value-laden and relevant is indispensable. In this chapter, we'll navigate through the tips for generating content that not only grasps attention but persuades and converts, as well as explore the varied content types apt for affiliate marketing.

Tips for Creating Engaging & Persuasive Content

Understand Your Audience: Knowing your audience is paramount. Understand their needs, preferences, challenges, and the solutions they seek. This understanding allows you to craft content that resonates, offering value that keeps them engaged and motivated to take action.

Deliver Value: Your content should offer tangible value to your audience, providing answers, solutions, or valuable insights related to your niche. Value-driven content builds trust and positions you as an authority, making your promotional efforts more effective.

Craft Compelling Calls to Action (CTAs): Effective CTAs guide your audience on what to do next. Whether it's to read more, sign up, or make a purchase, clear and compelling CTAs are crucial for driving conversions.

Utilize Visuals: Incorporating images, infographics, or videos can enhance the appeal and impact of your content, making it more engaging and shareable.

Be Authentic & Transparent: Authenticity builds trust. Be honest about the products you're promoting, sharing both pros and cons. Transparency about your affiliate relationship is also important, as it fosters trust with your audience.

Content Types Suitable for Affiliate Marketing

Blog Posts: Blogs are versatile and can cover product reviews, how-to guides, or listicles of top products in your niche. With SEO optimization, they can drive organic traffic to your site, increasing visibility and conversion opportunities.

Videos: Videos can offer product demonstrations, reviews, or tutorials, providing a dynamic and engaging way for your audience to consume content. Platforms like YouTube are ideal for video content.

Social Media Updates: Social media platforms are excellent for promoting affiliate products due to their wide reach and the ability to engage directly with your audience. Craft posts that are shareable and attention-grabbing.

Email Newsletters: Email marketing allows you to send personalized content directly to your subscribers' inboxes, promoting products in a more targeted manner. It's ideal for building and nurturing relationships with your audience.

Resource Pages: These are pages on your website where you list valuable resources, tools, or products related to your niche. Including affiliate links on these pages can generate passive income.

Creating Content that Converts

Crafting content that is not only engaging but also converts requires a blend of understanding your audience, delivering value, and using the appropriate format and platform to communicate your message. Always approach content creation with the end goal in mind—providing value that leads to conversions.

As we delve deeper into "A Beginner's to Successful Affiliate Marketing from Home: Passive Income Made Simple", subsequent sections will further equip you with the strategies and insights necessary for success, bringing you closer to realizing your goal of earning between $2k to $20k a month or more from the comfort of your home through affiliate marketing. The journey of mastery continues with every page!

Step 6: Utilizing Seo Strategies

In the realm of affiliate marketing, visibility is key, and SEO plays an indispensable role in ensuring your content not only reaches the widest audience but engages individuals who are genuinely interested in your niche. SEO, or Search Engine Optimization, enhances the visibility and searchability of your content online, making it a crucial tool in your affiliate marketing arsenal. In this section, we shall explore basic SEO strategies that are not just applicable but essential for affiliate marketing success.

Basic SEO Strategies for Affiliate Marketing

Keyword Research: Understanding what your target audience is searching for online is fundamental. Implement tools like Google Keyword Planner, Ahrefs, or SEMrush to discover relevant keywords in your niche. Incorporate these keywords naturally into your content to increase its visibility and relevance.

On-Page SEO: This involves optimizing individual pages on your website to improve their ranking and earn more relevant traffic. Essential elements include using keywords in strategic locations like the title, headers, and meta descriptions, as well as creating quality content and incorporating relevant internal and external links.

Quality Content: As aforementioned, content is paramount. Search engines favor content that is valuable, relevant, and fresh. Consistently producing quality content not only engages your audience but also improves your site's SEO.

Link Building: Links are a major factor used by search engines to rank websites. Cultivate backlinks from reputable sites in your niche. These links enhance the credibility and authority of your site, improving its ranking on search engine results pages (SERPs).

User Experience: A website that's easy to navigate and user-friendly is favored by search engines. Ensure your site is responsive (mobile-friendly), has a clean design, and loads quickly to offer a superior user experience.

Analytics: Utilize tools like Google Analytics to monitor and analyze your website's performance. Understand which pages are driving traffic, the keywords that users are searching for, and how long they stay on your site. This data is invaluable in refining your SEO strategies over time.

SEO: A Continuous Effort

It's vital to note that SEO isn't a 'set-and-forget' endeavor; it requires continuous effort and adaptation to the ever-evolving algorithms of search engines. Keeping abreast of the latest SEO trends and implementing them in your strategy ensures your affiliate marketing content remains visible and competitive.

By diligently applying these SEO basics, you enhance the visibility and accessibility of your affiliate links, driving traffic that is not just high in volume but also relevant and likely to convert. The journey through "A Beginner's Guide to Successful Affiliate Marketing from Home: Passive Income Made Simple" continues, with each page unfolding essential strategies and insights designed to guide you towards earning $2k to $20k a month or more from home through affiliate marketing. Stay engaged as we delve deeper into the roadmap to affiliate marketing mastery!

Step 7: Social Media & Email Marketing

Harnessing the potent combination of social media and email marketing can significantly amplify your affiliate marketing efforts. While social media provides extensive reach and dynamic engagement opportunities, email marketing facilitates direct, personalized communication with your audience. In this section, we'll explore how to adeptly utilize both tools to broaden your influence and foster sales in the affiliate marketing landscape.

Social Media for Affiliate Marketing

Select Relevant Platforms: Different social media platforms attract distinct audience demographics. Identify where your target audience predominantly resides and focus your efforts there, whether it's on Facebook, Instagram, Twitter, LinkedIn, Pinterest, or others.

Engage Your Audience: Interaction is the lifeblood of social media. Engage with your audience through comments, messages, and by participating in groups or forums related to your niche.

Share Valuable Content: Consistently post content that is informative, entertaining, or inspirational. Value-driven posts establish trust and authority with your audience.

Use Visuals: Visual content, including images, infographics, and videos, tends to garner more engagement. Incorporate eye-catching visuals to complement and enhance your promotional posts.

Include Clear CTAs: Guide your audience on the next steps to take, whether it's visiting your website, signing up for a newsletter, or checking out a product.

Email Marketing for Affiliate Marketing

Build Your List: Having a list of subscribers is vital for successful email marketing. Utilize your website, social media platforms, or other channels to encourage sign-ups.

Segment Your List: Not all subscribers have the same needs or interests. Segment your list to send tailored content that resonates with different audience groups.

Craft Compelling Content: Write engaging, concise, and valuable content. A compelling subject line is crucial to encourage opens, while the email body should provide value and a clear call to action.

Optimize for Mobile: Many users access their emails via mobile devices. Ensure your emails are mobile-friendly to provide a seamless experience for all recipients.

Monitor & Analyze: Track the performance of your email campaigns, paying attention to open rates, click-through rates, and conversions to understand what works best and refine your strategy accordingly.

Combining Social Media and Email Marketing

Cross-Promotion: Promote your email sign-up through social media and vice versa. This cross-promotion expands your reach on both platforms.

Consistent Messaging: Maintain consistency in your messaging across both channels to reinforce your brand identity and promotional campaigns.

Leverage User-Generated Content: Showcase content created by your followers or subscribers on both platforms, fostering community engagement and social proof.

Final Thoughts

Effectively integrating social media and email marketing within your affiliate marketing strategy can exponentially increase your reach and conversion potential. By understanding and applying the principles outlined in this section, you set the stage for a more interactive and profitable affiliate marketing endeavor.

The journey through "A Beginner's Guide to Successful Affiliate Marketing from Home: Passive Income Made Simple" unfolds further insights and actionable strategies, edging you closer to your goal of generating $2k to $20k a month or more from home. Each subsequent page is a step towards mastering affiliate marketing—stay tuned for more invaluable insights and guidance!

Step 8: Analyzing & Improving Performance

For sustained success in affiliate marketing, regularly analyzing and refining your performance is non-negotiable. Understanding the dynamics of your traffic, the effectiveness of your content, and the responsiveness of your audience allows you to sharpen your strategies, making them more attuned to your audience's needs and preferences. In this chapter, we'll delve into the essentials of performance analysis and improvement in affiliate marketing.

Analyzing Affiliate Marketing Performance

Monitor Traffic: Tracking the volume and sources of traffic to your affiliate content provides insights into your audience's behavior and the effectiveness of your promotional channels.

Click-Through Rates (CTR): CTR represents the percentage of viewers who click on your affiliate links relative to the total who viewed the content. A higher CTR indicates more effective and engaging content.

Conversion Rates: The conversion rate showcases the percentage of click-throughs that result in a sale. Understanding your conversion rates helps in identifying which products or services resonate most with your audience.

Revenue: Regularly track your earnings from each affiliate link to understand which products or services are most lucrative.

User Engagement: Measure how users interact with your content, considering metrics like page views, time spent on the site, bounce rates, and social shares.

Tips for Improving Your Campaigns

Refine Content: Based on your analysis, adjust your content to better cater to your audience. This might involve improving the clarity, adding more value, incorporating engaging visuals, or optimizing for SEO.

Test Different Offers: Experiment with promoting different products or services to understand which ones your audience prefers and which bring in higher commissions.

Enhance Calls-to-Action: If your CTR is low, consider revising your calls-to-action to make them more compelling and noticeable.

Optimize Conversion Funnel: Streamline the path from viewing content to completing a purchase to make it as smooth and straightforward as possible for users.

Adjust Marketing Channels: Based on the performance of different marketing channels, redistribute your efforts and resources to focus on the most effective ones.

Seek Feedback: Actively seek feedback from your audience regarding your content and offers. This direct insight can guide improvements and deepen your connection with your audience.

Continuous Learning: Stay updated on the latest trends, tools, and best practices in affiliate marketing and apply this knowledge to enhance your campaigns.

Continuous Improvement

Performance analysis and improvement should be ongoing processes in your affiliate marketing journey. As the digital landscape and audience preferences continuously evolve, staying adaptive and proactive in refining your strategies is vital for sustained success.

With the insights and techniques outlined in "A Beginner's Guide to Successful Affiliate Marketing from Home: Passive Income Made Simple", you are well-positioned to engage in a process of continual learning and improvement, propelling you towards your goal of earning between $2k to $20k a month or more from home. As you turn to the final page, anticipate concluding remarks that encapsulate the guide's essence and illuminate the path ahead in your affiliate marketing adventure.

Conclusion & Next Steps

Embarking on the promising journey of affiliate marketing is indeed a venture filled with potential and excitement. With the right approach, informed strategies, and a diligent mindset, you are not just stepping into a field of opportunity, but positioning yourself for success and profitability. You've journeyed through selecting a profitable niche, aligning with fitting affiliate programs, crafting compelling content, employing SEO techniques, and maximizing the utility of social media and email marketing—all fundamental blocks building up to a thriving affiliate marketing career. Now, with these strategies at your fingertips, the stage is set; it's time to spring into action and commence your earning journey!

Key Points Recap:

Niche Selection: Your chosen niche is the canvas upon which you'll paint your affiliate marketing efforts. It should resonate with your interests and expertise, boasting demand and profitability.

Affiliate Programs: Engage with programs offering products aligning with your niche, backed by supportive and reliable structures.

Content Creation: Craft content that's engaging, valuable, and relevant, serving as a magnetic force drawing your audience in and guiding them towards conversions.

SEO Strategies: SEO is your ally in enhancing visibility, driving organic traffic to your content, and ultimately, your affiliate links.

Social Media & Email Marketing: These powerful tools amplify your reach and engagement, facilitating both broad and personalized communication with your audience.

Next Steps:

Implement Learned Strategies: Begin applying the strategies and insights garnered from this guide. Implementation is where knowledge transforms into results.

Track & Analyze: Regularly monitor your performance, scrutinizing traffic, engagement, and conversion metrics to understand your campaign's strengths and areas needing improvement.

Refine & Optimize: Based on your analysis, make necessary adjustments to your content, promotional strategies, and engagement techniques to enhance performance.

Stay Updated: Affiliate marketing is dynamic; stay informed on emerging trends, tools, and best practices within the industry.
Invest in Learning: Consider enrolling in affiliate marketing courses, joining relevant forums and communities, and consistently consuming content from established affiliate marketers to deepen your knowledge and skills.

Take Action: The most critical step is to take action. Start now, learn as you go, and don't be afraid to make mistakes—they're invaluable learning opportunities.

Final Thoughts
As we conclude "A Beginner's Guide to Successful Affiliate Marketing from Home: Passive Income Made Simple", remember that the affiliate marketing journey is one of continuous learning and adaptation. Each step taken and every strategy implemented brings you closer to realizing your financial goals. With dedication, effort, and a commitment to applying and refining the strategies shared in this guide, the path ahead is bright with

the promise of success and the potential to earn from $2k to $20k a month or more from home. Here's to your success in the exhilarating realm of affiliate marketing!

www.ingramcontent.com/pod-product-compliance
Lightning Source LLC
Chambersburg PA
CBHW072228290526
45794CB00007B/2937